"A crazy blessed life doesn't happen by accident. It is created out of planning, passion, and persistence."

BASED ON THE MOM MASTERY METHOD™
CREATED BY HANNAH KEELEY

Master Mom Manifesto

My name is _____

and I'm a Master Mom.

I'm one mom of many who are quietly changing the world.

We're not marching in protests or setting up media campaigns.
We don't have time for that.

While other moms are making excuses, we're getting results.
While other moms are dreaming, we're awake doing.
While they're griping, we're grinding.
While they complain, we conquer.

We don't believe in being "just" a mom (whatever that means).
We believe moms are the critical element that determines the destiny of generations.

People shrug us off, heaven backs us up, and
hell is terrified of us.

We realize the power within us is greater than anything that can come at us, and because of this, we have the tendency to do pretty radical things. You can call us crazy, maniacs, rebels, but you can't call us average.

Tell us we can't do it, then move out of the way and watch.
Because we can do all things through the power at work in us
and through us.

We change the world as easily as we change diapers.

And we're not alone.

God has our back and the world is at our feet;
and we are stronger—together.

And we're growing—quickly.

We're Master Moms.

We don't allow excuses;
we push past them.
We don't hide from fear;
We rise above it.
We don't raise children;
We empower them.
We don't tolerate life.
We master it.

Step 1: MASSIVE ACTION

Let's face it. Planners don't work for most moms because they are not designed the way moms work. It's that simple. The Master Mom Planner solves this problem. We take it one quarter at a time--not too short, not too long. Each quarter gives us an opportunity to reassess our goals and the strategies we use to reach them.

The Master Mom Planner also strategically incorporates the Mom Mastery Method™ which I developed. This method is an incremental system that helps moms do the inside work that is required to live a life that is blessed like crazy. The method works. You just have to work the method. The Master Mom Planner lays it all out for you. Just plug in and go!

It's part planning system, part personal development, part calendar, but all YOU! So make it yours. Write, draw, erase, scratch out, decorate, change, dream, but most of all, do. Remember, sloppy success beats perfect failure.

Finally, I got your back.

STEP 1 of the Mom Mastery Method™ is MASSIVE ACTION, so let's get to it!

I created a free training based on the Mom Mastery Method™ to help you get the most of out of this planner. Take that fist step by going to the link below and getting plugged in.

www.hannahkeeley.com/plannertraining

Let's go! The abundant life God designed for you to live is waiting in these pages.

Hannah

Step 2: MOTIVATION

Use the following pages to form your vision for this quarter. Write, draw, or glue pics to describe what you want to be, do, and feel over the next three months. If you have goals from last quarter review them to assess if still applicable or if anything needs to be altered. Also, no need to get specific. This exercise is to determine your direction, not necessarily your path.

We're capturing a "snapshot" of where you want to go. You don't need to overanalyze this process. Just go with your gut. Instead of writing down the goals you think you should have, dig deep and capture how you want to feel and what you want to experience.

Not every category may apply to you, so just dive into the ones that do. And have fun!

The Six Pillars of Mom Mastery University:

1. Faith	your relationship with God
2. Family	marriage and parenting
3. Fortress	home maintenance
4. Finances	money management
5. Fitness	health and wellness
6. Freedom	personal development

Faith

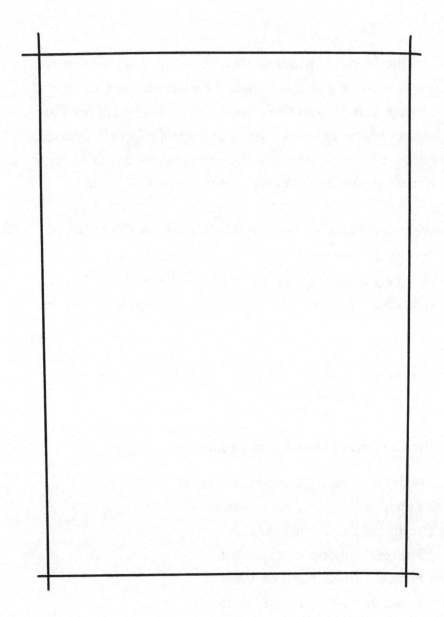

Family

Fortress

Finances

Fitness

Freedom

Step 3: MISSION

Now it's time to develop your mission for this quarter. This is where you take your vision and put some solid ground beneath it. Study each category that you just completed in Step 2: Motivation. What goals can you develop around the vision you created? Remember, moms can't create goals like other people.

We need to create **I.N.N.E.R. M.O.M.** goals:

I	Always begin your goals with "I" to make them more personal.
N	Now--Put your goals in the present as if they already happened.
N	Not Limited--Dream big! Don't put limits on what God can do.
E	Emotional--Add words that create positive emotion to your goals.
R	Reliant on God's Word--Find a promise to put with your goal.
M	Measurable--Get specific with your goals-- how much, by when?
O	Only Positives--Avoid the words "no" and "not."
M	Multiple Categories--Cover all the areas where you have impact.

Use the following pages to create your I.N.N.E.R. M.O.M. goals. Don't rush this process. It may take some time. If applicable, review last quarter's goals and see if they need to be altered in any way, abandoned because it no longer fits with your vision, or left off because you completed it and made it your "victory" instead of your "vision."

Faith

Family

Fortress

Finances

Fitness

Freedom

The Fab 5

Some goals are more powerful than others because they can serve to push all other goals forward. Review your goals and develop your "Fab 5," those 5 goals that if accomplished, you would consider this quarter (or even this year) a huge success! Shorten them to a brief sentence that you can write every single day and list them below:

MY Fab 5

1. _____
2. _____
3. _____
4. _____
5. _____

Step 4: MINDSET

Now you need to take your vision and create the mindset to make it happen. If you want to change the direction of your life, you need to change the declaration of your mouth.

Record your goals as vocal proclamations; create a daily routine to hear them and speak them out loud, then track your progress using the routine tracker from Step 6: Momentum.

Pro • Claim:
To take claim of something before it happens!

○ Check here when you have completed your proclamations.

Step 5: MAP

Analyze each goal and create a routine around it. Then record this routine in your MAP (Mundane Action Plan). This is also where you will keep track of any tasks you need to complete.

Your MAP is your new calendar! No more "to do" list!

- ☐ Commit to a daily AM and PM routine of planning and reviewing your MAP. Make it non-negotiable!

Step 6: MOMENTUM

You also have "My Routine Tracker. This is where you will keep track of your routines, giving yourself a check mark for each week you completed your routine. Or, go the extra mile and give yourself a gold star (we never grow out of those!).

It takes 21 days to develop a routine; so you have plenty of room to list them and track them for the entire quarter. There are spots for 12 weeks. At the end of the quarter, give yourself an assessment for your routines and use it to reward yourself or adapt the routines to fit your life better.

- ☐ Check here after you list all routines in your routine tracker.

AM AND PM ROUTINES

AM ROUTINES

You need to start your day and end your day in the most powerful and productive way possible. Use the areas below to create your ideal AM & PM Routines.

PM ROUTINES

MY Routine Tracker

#	ROUTINE	WK1	WK2	WK3	WK4	WK5	WK6
1							
2							
3							
4							
5							
6							
7							
8							
9							
10							
11							
12							
13							
14							
15							
16							
17							
18							
19							
20							
21							

Momentum

Write down all of your routines you are currently developing and give yourself a check (or even a gold star) on every week you follow through. Remember, the secret to your success is hidden within your daily routine!

	WK7	WK8	WK9	WK10	WK11	WK12	SCORE
1							
2							
3							
4							
5							
6							
7							
8							
9							
10							
11							
12							
13							
14							
15							
16							
17							
18							
19							
20							
21							

Step 7: MEDITATION

Prayer and meditation needs to be a daily routine (add it to your routine tracker). To help you maintain your prayer practice you will have a small area in your MAP to keep track of it.

You can download a FREE guided meditation by visiting
www.hannahkeeley.com/meditation

☐ Commit to making prayer and meditation a daily routine.

Step 8: MANIFESTATION

To create the crazy blessed life, you need to focus on the three aspects of Manifestation:

- Coaching
- Community
- Continuity

Make sure you **continue** your personal development through regular **coaching** and plugging in to a powerful and encouraging **community**. You will find all this and so much more inside Mom Mastery University.

Visit MomMastery.com and enroll now! You can also become a Mentor and create wealth by encouraging other moms just like you!

To help you contine the process of manifestation, you will have a small area in your MAP to keep track of it.

JULY 1   MY *Map*   ZONE

AGENDA	ACTIONS
6 am	
8 am	
9 am	
10 am	
11 am	
12 pm	
1 pm	
2 pm	
3 pm	
4 pm	
5 pm	
6 pm	
7 pm	
9 pm	

NOTES

○ AM *routine*   ○ PM *routine*

My "FAB 5" (AM)
1. _____
2. _____
3. _____
4. _____
5. _____

My "FAB 5" (PM)
1. _____
2. _____
3. _____
4. _____
5. _____

today's MEALS

Meditation

What do I need to release to God today?

What am I grateful for today? Why?

What am I hearing from God today?

My successes today _____
My challenges today _____

MANIFESTATION

Did I invest in my personal growth today? ○
Did I invest in the growth of others today? ○

| JULY 2 | MY Map | ZONE |

AGENDA

6 am
8 am
9 am
10 am
11 am
12 pm
1 pm
2 pm
3 pm
4 pm
5 pm
6 pm
7 pm
9 pm

ACTIONS

NOTES

○ AM *routine*   ○ PM *routine*

My "FAB 5" (AM)
1. _____
2. _____
3. _____
4. _____
5. _____

My "FAB 5" (PM)
1. _____
2. _____
3. _____
4. _____
5. _____

today's MEALS

Meditation

What do I need to release to God today?

What am I grateful for today? Why?

What am I hearing from God today?

My successes today _____
My challenges today _____

MANIFESTATION

Did I invest in my personal growth today? ○
Did I invest in the growth of others today? ○

JULY 3 **MY Map** ZONE

AGENDA

6 am
8 am
9 am
10 am
11 am
12 pm
1 pm
2 pm
3 pm
4 pm
5 pm
6 pm
7 pm
9 pm

ACTIONS

NOTES

○ AM *routine*   ○ PM *routine*

My "FAB 5" (AM)
1. _____
2. _____
3. _____
4. _____
5. _____

My "FAB 5" (PM)
1. _____
2. _____
3. _____
4. _____
5. _____

today's MEALS

Meditation

What do I need to release to God today?

What am I grateful for today? Why?

What am I hearing from God today?

My successes today _____
My challenges today _____

MANIFESTATION

Did I invest in my personal growth today? ○
Did I invest in the growth of others today? ○

| JULY 4 | MY *Map* | ZONE |

AGENDA

- 6 am
- 8 am
- 9 am
- 10 am
- 11 am
- 12 pm
- 1 pm
- 2 pm
- 3 pm
- 4 pm
- 5 pm
- 6 pm
- 7 pm
- 9 pm

ACTIONS

NOTES

◯ AM *routine*   ◯ PM *routine*

My "FAB 5" (AM)
1. ___
2. ___
3. ___
4. ___
5. ___

My "FAB 5" (PM)
1. ___
2. ___
3. ___
4. ___
5. ___

today's MEALS

Meditation

What do I need to release to God today?

What am I grateful for today? Why?

What am I hearing from God today?

My successes today ___
My challenges today ___

MANIFESTATION

Did I invest in my personal growth today? ◯
Did I invest in the growth of others today? ◯

| JULY 5 |

MY Map

ZONE

AGENDA

6 am
8 am
9 am
10 am
11 am
12 pm
1 pm
2 pm
3 pm
4 pm
5 pm
6 pm
7 pm
9 pm

ACTIONS

NOTES

◯ AM *routine*   ◯ PM *routine*

My "FAB 5" (AM)
1. _____
2. _____
3. _____
4. _____
5. _____

My "FAB 5" (PM)
1. _____
2. _____
3. _____
4. _____
5. _____

today's MEALS

Meditation

What do I need to release to God today?
_____

What am I grateful for today? Why?
_____

What am I hearing from God today?
_____

My successes today _____
My challenges today _____

MANIFESTATION

Did I invest in my personal growth today? ◯
Did I invest in the growth of others today? ◯

| JULY 6 | MY Map | ZONE |

AGENDA | ACTIONS

6 am

8 am

9 am

10 am

11 am

12 pm

1 pm

2 pm

3 pm

4 pm

5 pm

6 pm

7 pm

9 pm

NOTES

○ AM *routine*   ○ PM *routine*

My "FAB 5" (AM)
1. _____
2. _____
3. _____
4. _____
5. _____

My "FAB 5" (PM)
1. _____
2. _____
3. _____
4. _____
5. _____

today's MEALS

Meditation

What do I need to release to God today?

What am I grateful for today? Why?

What am I hearing from God today?

My successes today _____
My challenges today _____

MANIFESTATION

Did I invest in my personal growth today? ○
Did I invest in the growth of others today? ○

JULY 7

MY *Map*

ZONE

AGENDA

6 am
8 am
9 am
10 am
11 am
12 pm
1 pm
2 pm
3 pm
4 pm
5 pm
6 pm
7 pm
9 pm

ACTIONS

NOTES

○ AM *routine*   ○ PM *routine*

My "FAB 5" (AM)
1.
2.
3.
4.
5.

My "FAB 5" (PM)
1.
2.
3.
4.
5.

today's MEALS

Meditation

What do I need to release to God today?

What am I grateful for today? Why?

What am I hearing from God today?

My successes today _____
My challenges today _____

MANIFESTATION

Did I invest in my personal growth today? ○
Did I invest in the growth of others today? ○

JULY 8 — MY Map — ZONE

AGENDA

6 am
8 am
9 am
10 am
11 am
12 pm
1 pm
2 pm
3 pm
4 pm
5 pm
6 pm
7 pm
9 pm

ACTIONS

NOTES

◯ AM *routine*   ◯ PM *routine*

My "FAB 5" (AM)
1. _____
2. _____
3. _____
4. _____
5. _____

My "FAB 5" (PM)
1. _____
2. _____
3. _____
4. _____
5. _____

today's MEALS

Meditation

What do I need to release to God today?

What am I grateful for today? Why?

What am I hearing from God today?

My successes today _____
My challenges today _____

MANIFESTATION

Did I invest in my personal growth today? ◯
Did I invest in the growth of others today? ◯

| JULY 9 | MY *Map* | ZONE |

AGENDA

- 6 am
- 8 am
- 9 am
- 10 am
- 11 am
- 12 pm
- 1 pm
- 2 pm
- 3 pm
- 4 pm
- 5 pm
- 6 pm
- 7 pm
- 9 pm

ACTIONS

NOTES

○ AM *routine*   ○ PM *routine*

My "FAB 5" (AM)
1. _____
2. _____
3. _____
4. _____
5. _____

My "FAB 5" (PM)
1. _____
2. _____
3. _____
4. _____
5. _____

today's MEALS

Meditation
What do I need to release to God today?

What am I grateful for today? Why?

What am I hearing from God today?

My successes today _____
My challenges today _____

MANIFESTATION

Did I invest in my personal growth today? ○
Did I invest in the growth of others today? ○

MY Map

JULY 10

ZONE

AGENDA

- 6 am
- 8 am
- 9 am
- 10 am
- 11 am
- 12 pm
- 1 pm
- 2 pm
- 3 pm
- 4 pm
- 5 pm
- 6 pm
- 7 pm
- 9 pm

ACTIONS

NOTES

◯ AM *routine*   ◯ PM *routine*

My "FAB 5" (AM)
1. _____
2. _____
3. _____
4. _____
5. _____

My "FAB 5" (PM)
1. _____
2. _____
3. _____
4. _____
5. _____

today's MEALS

Meditation

What do I need to release to God today?

What am I grateful for today? Why?

What am I hearing from God today?

My successes today _____
My challenges today _____

MANIFESTATION

Did I invest in my personal growth today? ◯
Did I invest in the growth of others today? ◯

| JULY 11 | MY *Map* | ZONE |

AGENDA	ACTIONS
6 am	
8 am	
9 am	
10 am	
11 am	
12 pm	
1 pm	
2 pm	
3 pm	
4 pm	
5 pm	
6 pm	
7 pm	
9 pm	

NOTES

○ AM *routine*   ○ PM *routine*

My "FAB 5" (AM)
1. _____
2. _____
3. _____
4. _____
5. _____

My "FAB 5" (PM)
1. _____
2. _____
3. _____
4. _____
5. _____

today's MEALS

Meditation

What do I need to release to God today?

What am I grateful for today? Why?

What am I hearing from God today?

My successes today _____
My challenges today _____

MANIFESTATION

Did I invest in my personal growth today? ○
Did I invest in the growth of others today? ○

| JULY 12 |

MY Map

ZONE

AGENDA	ACTIONS
6 am	
8 am	
9 am	
10 am	
11 am	
12 pm	
1 pm	
2 pm	
3 pm	
4 pm	
5 pm	
6 pm	
7 pm	
9 pm	

NOTES

○ AM *routine* ○ PM *routine*

My "FAB 5" (AM)
1. _____
2. _____
3. _____
4. _____
5. _____

My "FAB 5" (PM)
1. _____
2. _____
3. _____
4. _____
5. _____

today's MEALS

Meditation

What do I need to release to God today?
_____

What am I grateful for today? Why?
_____

What am I hearing from God today?
_____

My successes today _____
My challenges today _____

MANIFESTATION

Did I invest in my personal growth today? ○
Did I invest in the growth of others today? ○

| JULY 13 | MY *Map* | ZONE |

AGENDA

6 am
8 am
9 am
10 am
11 am
12 pm
1 pm
2 pm
3 pm
4 pm
5 pm
6 pm
7 pm
9 pm

ACTIONS

NOTES

◯ AM *routine*   ◯ PM *routine*

My "FAB 5" (AM)
1. ___
2. ___
3. ___
4. ___
5. ___

My "FAB 5" (PM)
1. ___
2. ___
3. ___
4. ___
5. ___

today's MEALS

Meditation

What do I need to release to God today? ___

What am I grateful for today? Why? ___

What am I hearing from God today? ___

My successes today ___
My challenges today ___

MANIFESTATION

Did I invest in my personal growth today? ◯

Did I invest in the growth of others today? ◯

(JULY 14)   MY *Map*   ZONE ( )

AGENDA

6 am
8 am
9 am
10 am
11 am
12 pm
1 pm
2 pm
3 pm
4 pm
5 pm
6 pm
7 pm
9 pm

ACTIONS

NOTES

○ AM *routine*   ○ PM *routine*

My "FAB 5" (AM)
1. _____
2. _____
3. _____
4. _____
5. _____

My "FAB 5" (PM)
1. _____
2. _____
3. _____
4. _____
5. _____

today's MEALS

Meditation

What do I need to release to God today?

What am I grateful for today? Why?

What am I hearing from God today?

My successes today _____
My challenges today _____

MANIFESTATION

Did I invest in my personal growth today? ○
Did I invest in the growth of others today? ○

| JULY 15 | MY *Map* | ZONE |

AGENDA	ACTIONS
6 am	
8 am	
9 am	
10 am	
11 am	
12 pm	
1 pm	
2 pm	
3 pm	
4 pm	
5 pm	
6 pm	
7 pm	
9 pm	

NOTES

○ AM *routine* ○ PM *routine*

My "FAB 5" (AM)

1. _____
2. _____
3. _____
4. _____
5. _____

My "FAB 5" (PM)

1. _____
2. _____
3. _____
4. _____
5. _____

today's MEALS

Meditation

What do I need to release to God today?

What am I grateful for today? Why?

What am I hearing from God today?

My successes today _____

My challenges today _____

MANIFESTATION

Did I invest in my personal growth today? ○

Did I invest in the growth of others today? ○

| JULY 16 | MY *Map* | ZONE |

AGENDA | ACTIONS

6 am

8 am

9 am

10 am

11 am

12 pm

1 pm

2 pm

3 pm

4 pm

5 pm

6 pm

7 pm

9 pm

NOTES

◯ AM *routine* ◯ PM *routine*

My "FAB 5" (AM)
1. _____
2. _____
3. _____
4. _____
5. _____

My "FAB 5" (PM)
1. _____
2. _____
3. _____
4. _____
5. _____

today's MEALS

Meditation

What do I need to release to God today? _____

What am I grateful for today? Why? _____

What am I hearing from God today? _____

My successes today _____
My challenges today _____

MANIFESTATION

Did I invest in my personal growth today? ◯
Did I invest in the growth of others today? ◯

JULY 17

MY Map

ZONE

AGENDA

6 am
8 am
9 am
10 am
11 am
12 pm
1 pm
2 pm
3 pm
4 pm
5 pm
6 pm
7 pm
9 pm

ACTIONS

NOTES

◯ AM *routine*   ◯ PM *routine*

My "FAB 5" (AM)
1. _____
2. _____
3. _____
4. _____
5. _____

My "FAB 5" (PM)
1. _____
2. _____
3. _____
4. _____
5. _____

today's MEALS

Meditation

What do I need to release to God today?

What am I grateful for today? Why?

What am I hearing from God today?

My successes today _____
My challenges today _____

MANIFESTATION

Did I invest in my personal growth today? ◯
Did I invest in the growth of others today? ◯

| JULY 18 | MY *Map* | ZONE |

AGENDA

- 6 am
- 8 am
- 9 am
- 10 am
- 11 am
- 12 pm
- 1 pm
- 2 pm
- 3 pm
- 4 pm
- 5 pm
- 6 pm
- 7 pm
- 9 pm

ACTIONS

NOTES

○ AM *routine*   ○ PM *routine*

My "FAB 5" (AM)
1. _____
2. _____
3. _____
4. _____
5. _____

My "FAB 5" (PM)
1. _____
2. _____
3. _____
4. _____
5. _____

today's MEALS

Meditation

What do I need to release to God today?

What am I grateful for today? Why?

What am I hearing from God today?

My successes today _____
My challenges today _____

MANIFESTATION

Did I invest in my personal growth today? ○
Did I invest in the growth of others today? ○

63

JULY 19

MY *Map*

ZONE ⬯

AGENDA	ACTIONS
6 am	
8 am	
9 am	
10 am	
11 am	
12 pm	
1 pm	
2 pm	
3 pm	
4 pm	
5 pm	
6 pm	
7 pm	
9 pm	

NOTES

◯ AM *routine*   ◯ PM *routine*

My "FAB 5" (AM)
1. ___
2. ___
3. ___
4. ___
5. ___

My "FAB 5" (PM)
1. ___
2. ___
3. ___
4. ___
5. ___

today's MEALS

Meditation

What do I need to release to God today?

What am I grateful for today? Why?

What am I hearing from God today?

My successes today ___
My challenges today ___

MANIFESTATION

Did I invest in my personal growth today? ◯
Did I invest in the growth of others today? ◯

JULY 20

MY *Map*

ZONE

AGENDA

6 am
8 am
9 am
10 am
11 am
12 pm
1 pm
2 pm
3 pm
4 pm
5 pm
6 pm
7 pm
9 pm

ACTIONS

NOTES

○ AM *routine*   ○ PM *routine*

My "FAB 5" (AM)
1. _____
2. _____
3. _____
4. _____
5. _____

My "FAB 5" (PM)
1. _____
2. _____
3. _____
4. _____
5. _____

today's MEALS

Meditation

What do I need to release to God today?

What am I grateful for today? Why?

What am I hearing from God today?

My successes today _____
My challenges today _____

MANIFESTATION

Did I invest in my personal growth today? ○
Did I invest in the growth of others today? ○

| JULY 21 | MY *Map* | ZONE |

AGENDA

6 am
8 am
9 am
10 am
11 am
12 pm
1 pm
2 pm
3 pm
4 pm
5 pm
6 pm
7 pm
9 pm

ACTIONS

NOTES

○ AM *routine*   ○ PM *routine*

My "FAB 5" (AM)
1. _____
2. _____
3. _____
4. _____
5. _____

My "FAB 5" (PM)
1. _____
2. _____
3. _____
4. _____
5. _____

today's MEALS

Meditation

What do I need to release to God today?
_____

What am I grateful for today? Why?
_____

What am I hearing from God today?
_____

My successes today _____
My challenges today _____

MANIFESTATION
─────────────

Did I invest in my personal growth today? ○
Did I invest in the growth of others today? ○

| JULY 22 | MY *Map* | ZONE |

AGENDA	ACTIONS
6 am	
8 am	
9 am	
10 am	
11 am	
12 pm	
1 pm	
2 pm	
3 pm	
4 pm	
5 pm	
6 pm	
7 pm	
9 pm	

NOTES

◯ AM *routine* ◯ PM *routine*

My "FAB 5" (AM)
1. _____
2. _____
3. _____
4. _____
5. _____

My "FAB 5" (PM)
1. _____
2. _____
3. _____
4. _____
5. _____

today's MEALS

Meditation

What do I need to release to God today?

What am I grateful for today? Why?

What am I hearing from God today?

My successes today _____
My challenges today _____

MANIFESTATION

Did I invest in my personal growth today? ◯
Did I invest in the growth of others today? ◯

71

JULY 23

MY *Map*

ZONE

AGENDA	ACTIONS
6 am	
8 am	
9 am	
10 am	
11 am	
12 pm	
1 pm	
2 pm	
3 pm	
4 pm	
5 pm	
6 pm	
7 pm	
9 pm	

NOTES

○ AM *routine*   ○ PM *routine*

My "FAB 5" (AM)
1. _____
2. _____
3. _____
4. _____
5. _____

My "FAB 5" (PM)
1. _____
2. _____
3. _____
4. _____
5. _____

today's MEALS

Meditation

What do I need to release to God today?

What am I grateful for today? Why?

What am I hearing from God today?

My successes today _____
My challenges today _____

MANIFESTATION

Did I invest in my personal growth today? ○
Did I invest in the growth of others today? ○

| JULY 24 |

MY *Map*

ZONE

AGENDA

6 am
8 am
9 am
10 am
11 am
12 pm
1 pm
2 pm
3 pm
4 pm
5 pm
6 pm
7 pm
9 pm

ACTIONS

NOTES

○ AM *routine*   ○ PM *routine*

My "FAB 5" (AM)
1. _____
2. _____
3. _____
4. _____
5. _____

My "FAB 5" (PM)
1. _____
2. _____
3. _____
4. _____
5. _____

today's MEALS

Meditation

What do I need to release to God today?

What am I grateful for today? Why?

What am I hearing from God today?

My successes today _____
My challenges today _____

MANIFESTATION

Did I invest in my personal growth today? ○
Did I invest in the growth of others today? ○

| JULY 25 | MY *Map* | ZONE |

AGENDA

6 am
8 am
9 am
10 am
11 am
12 pm
1 pm
2 pm
3 pm
4 pm
5 pm
6 pm
7 pm
9 pm

ACTIONS

NOTES

○ AM *routine*   ○ PM *routine*

My "FAB 5" (AM)
1. _____
2. _____
3. _____
4. _____
5. _____

My "FAB 5" (PM)
1. _____
2. _____
3. _____
4. _____
5. _____

today's MEALS

Meditation

What do I need to release to God today?

What am I grateful for today? Why?

What am I hearing from God today?

My successes today _____
My challenges today _____

MANIFESTATION

Did I invest in my personal growth today? ○
Did I invest in the growth of others today? ○

JULY 26

MY *Map*

ZONE

AGENDA	ACTIONS
6 am	
8 am	
9 am	
10 am	
11 am	
12 pm	
1 pm	
2 pm	
3 pm	
4 pm	
5 pm	
6 pm	
7 pm	
9 pm	

NOTES

○ AM *routine*   ○ PM *routine*

My "FAB 5" (AM)
1.
2.
3.
4.
5.

My "FAB 5" (PM)
1.
2.
3.
4.
5.

today's MEALS

Meditation

What do I need to release to God today?

What am I grateful for today? Why?

What am I hearing from God today?

My successes today _____

My challenges today _____

MANIFESTATION

Did I invest in my personal growth today? ○

Did I invest in the growth of others today? ○

| JULY 27 | MY *Map* | ZONE |

AGENDA
- 6 am
- 8 am
- 9 am
- 10 am
- 11 am
- 12 pm
- 1 pm
- 2 pm
- 3 pm
- 4 pm
- 5 pm
- 6 pm
- 7 pm
- 9 pm

ACTIONS

NOTES

○ AM *routine*   ○ PM *routine*

My "FAB 5" (AM)
1. ___
2. ___
3. ___
4. ___
5. ___

My "FAB 5" (PM)
1. ___
2. ___
3. ___
4. ___
5. ___

today's MEALS

Meditation

What do I need to release to God today?

What am I grateful for today? Why?

What am I hearing from God today?

My successes today ___
My challenges today ___

MANIFESTATION

Did I invest in my personal growth today? ○
Did I invest in the growth of others today? ○

MY *Map*

JULY 28   ZONE ⬭

AGENDA   ACTIONS

- 6 am
- 8 am
- 9 am
- 10 am
- 11 am
- 12 pm
- 1 pm
- 2 pm
- 3 pm
- 4 pm
- 5 pm
- 6 pm
- 7 pm
- 9 pm

NOTES

◯ AM *routine*   ◯ PM *routine*

My "FAB 5" (AM)
1. _____
2. _____
3. _____
4. _____
5. _____

My "FAB 5" (PM)
1. _____
2. _____
3. _____
4. _____
5. _____

today's MEALS

Meditation

What do I need to release to God today?

What am I grateful for today? Why?

What am I hearing from God today?

My successes today _____

My challenges today _____

MANIFESTATION

Did I invest in my personal growth today? ◯

Did I invest in the growth of others today? ◯

| JULY 29 |

MY Map

ZONE

AGENDA

- 6 am
- 8 am
- 9 am
- 10 am
- 11 am
- 12 pm
- 1 pm
- 2 pm
- 3 pm
- 4 pm
- 5 pm
- 6 pm
- 7 pm
- 9 pm

ACTIONS

NOTES

○ AM *routine*   ○ PM *routine*

My "FAB 5" (AM)
1. _____
2. _____
3. _____
4. _____
5. _____

My "FAB 5" (PM)
1. _____
2. _____
3. _____
4. _____
5. _____

today's MEALS

Meditation

What do I need to release to God today?

What am I grateful for today? Why?

What am I hearing from God today?

My successes today _____
My challenges today _____

MANIFESTATION

Did I invest in my personal growth today? ○
Did I invest in the growth of others today? ○

JULY 30   MY *Map*   ZONE

AGENDA

- 6 am
- 8 am
- 9 am
- 10 am
- 11 am
- 12 pm
- 1 pm
- 2 pm
- 3 pm
- 4 pm
- 5 pm
- 6 pm
- 7 pm
- 9 pm

ACTIONS

NOTES

○ AM *routine*   ○ PM *routine*

My "FAB 5" (AM)
1. _____
2. _____
3. _____
4. _____
5. _____

My "FAB 5" (PM)
1. _____
2. _____
3. _____
4. _____
5. _____

today's MEALS

Meditation

What do I need to release to God today?

What am I grateful for today? Why?

What am I hearing from God today?

My successes today _____
My challenges today _____

MANIFESTATION

Did I invest in my personal growth today? ○
Did I invest in the growth of others today? ○

JULY 31

MY Map

ZONE

AGENDA

6 am
8 am
9 am
10 am
11 am
12 pm
1 pm
2 pm
3 pm
4 pm
5 pm
6 pm
7 pm
9 pm

ACTIONS

NOTES

○ AM *routine*   ○ PM *routine*

My "FAB 5" (AM)
1. _____
2. _____
3. _____
4. _____
5. _____

My "FAB 5" (PM)
1. _____
2. _____
3. _____
4. _____
5. _____

today's MEALS

Meditation

What do I need to release to God today?

What am I grateful for today? Why?

What am I hearing from God today?

My successes today _____
My challenges today _____

MANIFESTATION

Did I invest in my personal growth today? ○
Did I invest in the growth of others today? ○

| AUG 1 | MY *Map* | ZONE |

AGENDA

- 6 am
- 8 am
- 9 am
- 10 am
- 11 am
- 12 pm
- 1 pm
- 2 pm
- 3 pm
- 4 pm
- 5 pm
- 6 pm
- 7 pm
- 9 pm

ACTIONS

NOTES

◯ AM *routine*   ◯ PM *routine*

My "FAB 5" (AM)
1. _____
2. _____
3. _____
4. _____
5. _____

My "FAB 5" (PM)
1. _____
2. _____
3. _____
4. _____
5. _____

today's MEALS

Meditation

What do I need to release to God today?

What am I grateful for today? Why?

What am I hearing from God today?

My successes today _____

My challenges today _____

MANIFESTATION

Did I invest in my personal growth today? ◯

Did I invest in the growth of others today? ◯

MY Map

AUG 2   ZONE

AGENDA

- 6 am
- 8 am
- 9 am
- 10 am
- 11 am
- 12 pm
- 1 pm
- 2 pm
- 3 pm
- 4 pm
- 5 pm
- 6 pm
- 7 pm
- 9 pm

ACTIONS

NOTES

○ AM *routine*   ○ PM *routine*

My "FAB 5" (AM)
1.
2.
3.
4.
5.

My "FAB 5" (PM)
1.
2.
3.
4.
5.

today's MEALS

Meditation

What do I need to release to God today?

What am I grateful for today? Why?

What am I hearing from God today?

My successes today

My challenges today

MANIFESTATION

Did I invest in my personal growth today? ○

Did I invest in the growth of others today? ○

| AUG 3 | MY *Map* | ZONE |

AGENDA	ACTIONS
6 am	
8 am	
9 am	
10 am	
11 am	
12 pm	
1 pm	
2 pm	
3 pm	
4 pm	
5 pm	
6 pm	
7 pm	
9 pm	

NOTES

○ AM *routine*   ○ PM *routine*

My "FAB 5" (AM)
1. ___
2. ___
3. ___
4. ___
5. ___

My "FAB 5" (PM)
1. ___
2. ___
3. ___
4. ___
5. ___

today's MEALS

Meditation

What do I need to release to God today?

What am I grateful for today? Why?

What am I hearing from God today?

My successes today ___
My challenges today ___

MANIFESTATION

Did I invest in my personal growth today? ○
Did I invest in the growth of others today? ○

| AUG 4 | MY *Map* | ZONE |

AGENDA

6 am
8 am
9 am
10 am
11 am
12 pm
1 pm
2 pm
3 pm
4 pm
5 pm
6 pm
7 pm
9 pm

ACTIONS

NOTES

○ AM *routine*   ○ PM *routine*

My "FAB 5" (AM)
1. _____
2. _____
3. _____
4. _____
5. _____

My "FAB 5" (PM)
1. _____
2. _____
3. _____
4. _____
5. _____

today's MEALS

Meditation

What do I need to release to God today?

What am I grateful for today? Why?

What am I hearing from God today?

My successes today _____
My challenges today _____

MANIFESTATION

Did I invest in my personal growth today? ○
Did I invest in the growth of others today? ○

MY Map

AUG 5   ZONE

AGENDA

- 6 am
- 8 am
- 9 am
- 10 am
- 11 am
- 12 pm
- 1 pm
- 2 pm
- 3 pm
- 4 pm
- 5 pm
- 6 pm
- 7 pm
- 9 pm

ACTIONS

NOTES

○ AM *routine*   ○ PM *routine*

My "FAB 5" (AM)
1.
2.
3.
4.
5.

My "FAB 5" (PM)
1.
2.
3.
4.
5.

today's MEALS

Meditation

What do I need to release to God today?

What am I grateful for today? Why?

What am I hearing from God today?

My successes today
My challenges today

MANIFESTATION

Did I invest in my personal growth today? ○
Did I invest in the growth of others today? ○

| AUG 6 |

MY *Map*

ZONE

AGENDA	ACTIONS
6 am	
8 am	
9 am	
10 am	
11 am	
12 pm	
1 pm	
2 pm	
3 pm	
4 pm	
5 pm	
6 pm	
7 pm	
9 pm	

NOTES

○ AM *routine*   ○ PM *routine*

My "FAB 5" (AM)
1. _____
2. _____
3. _____
4. _____
5. _____

My "FAB 5" (PM)
1. _____
2. _____
3. _____
4. _____
5. _____

today's MEALS

Meditation

What do I need to release to God today?

What am I grateful for today? Why?

What am I hearing from God today?

My successes today _____
My challenges today _____

MANIFESTATION

Did I invest in my personal growth today? ○
Did I invest in the growth of others today? ○

| AUG 7 | MY Map | ZONE |

AGENDA / ACTIONS

- 6 am
- 8 am
- 9 am
- 10 am
- 11 am
- 12 pm
- 1 pm
- 2 pm
- 3 pm
- 4 pm
- 5 pm
- 6 pm
- 7 pm
- 9 pm

NOTES

◯ AM *routine*   ◯ PM *routine*

My "FAB 5" (AM)
1. _____
2. _____
3. _____
4. _____
5. _____

My "FAB 5" (PM)
1. _____
2. _____
3. _____
4. _____
5. _____

today's MEALS

Meditation

What do I need to release to God today?
_____

What am I grateful for today? Why?
_____

What am I hearing from God today?
_____

My successes today _____
My challenges today _____

MANIFESTATION

Did I invest in my personal growth today? ◯
Did I invest in the growth of others today? ◯

(AUG 8)

MY Map

ZONE ( )

AGENDA

6 am
8 am
9 am
10 am
11 am
12 pm
1 pm
2 pm
3 pm
4 pm
5 pm
6 pm
7 pm
9 pm

ACTIONS

NOTES

○ AM *routine*   ○ PM *routine*

My "FAB 5" (AM)
1. _____
2. _____
3. _____
4. _____
5. _____

My "FAB 5" (PM)
1. _____
2. _____
3. _____
4. _____
5. _____

today's MEALS

Meditation

What do I need to release to God today?

What am I grateful for today? Why?

What am I hearing from God today?

My successes today _____
My challenges today _____

MANIFESTATION

Did I invest in my personal growth today? ○
Did I invest in the growth of others today? ○

| AUG 9 |

MY *Map*

ZONE

AGENDA

6 am
8 am
9 am
10 am
11 am
12 pm
1 pm
2 pm
3 pm
4 pm
5 pm
6 pm
7 pm
9 pm

ACTIONS

NOTES

○ AM *routine*   ○ PM *routine*

My "FAB 5" (AM)
1. ___
2. ___
3. ___
4. ___
5. ___

My "FAB 5" (PM)
1. ___
2. ___
3. ___
4. ___
5. ___

today's MEALS

Meditation

What do I need to release to God today?

What am I grateful for today? Why?

What am I hearing from God today?

My successes today ___
My challenges today ___

MANIFESTATION

Did I invest in my personal growth today? ○
Did I invest in the growth of others today? ○

MY Map

AUG 10

ZONE

AGENDA

6 am
8 am
9 am
10 am
11 am
12 pm
1 pm
2 pm
3 pm
4 pm
5 pm
6 pm
7 pm
9 pm

ACTIONS

NOTES

○ AM *routine*   ○ PM *routine*

My "FAB 5" (AM)
1. ___
2. ___
3. ___
4. ___
5. ___

My "FAB 5" (PM)
1. ___
2. ___
3. ___
4. ___
5. ___

today's MEALS

Meditation

What do I need to release to God today?

What am I grateful for today? Why?

What am I hearing from God today?

My successes today ___
My challenges today ___

MANIFESTATION

Did I invest in my personal growth today? ○
Did I invest in the growth of others today? ○

| AUG 11 | MY *Map* | ZONE |

AGENDA

6 am
8 am
9 am
10 am
11 am
12 pm
1 pm
2 pm
3 pm
4 pm
5 pm
6 pm
7 pm
9 pm

ACTIONS

NOTES

○ AM *routine*   ○ PM *routine*

My "FAB 5" (AM)
1. _____
2. _____
3. _____
4. _____
5. _____

My "FAB 5" (PM)
1. _____
2. _____
3. _____
4. _____
5. _____

today's MEALS

Meditation

What do I need to release to God today?

What am I grateful for today? Why?

What am I hearing from God today?

My successes today _____
My challenges today _____

MANIFESTATION

Did I invest in my personal growth today? ○
Did I invest in the growth of others today? ○

MY Map

AUG 12 ZONE

AGENDA

- 6 am
- 8 am
- 9 am
- 10 am
- 11 am
- 12 pm
- 1 pm
- 2 pm
- 3 pm
- 4 pm
- 5 pm
- 6 pm
- 7 pm
- 9 pm

ACTIONS

NOTES

○ AM *routine*   ○ PM *routine*

My "FAB 5" (AM)
1. ___
2. ___
3. ___
4. ___
5. ___

My "FAB 5" (PM)
1. ___
2. ___
3. ___
4. ___
5. ___

today's MEALS

Meditation

What do I need to release to God today?

What am I grateful for today? Why?

What am I hearing from God today?

My successes today ___
My challenges today ___

MANIFESTATION

Did I invest in my personal growth today? ○
Did I invest in the growth of others today? ○

| AUG 13 | MY *Map* | ZONE |

AGENDA

- 6 am
- 8 am
- 9 am
- 10 am
- 11 am
- 12 pm
- 1 pm
- 2 pm
- 3 pm
- 4 pm
- 5 pm
- 6 pm
- 7 pm
- 9 pm

ACTIONS

NOTES

○ AM *routine*   ○ PM *routine*

My "FAB 5" (AM)
1. _____
2. _____
3. _____
4. _____
5. _____

My "FAB 5" (PM)
1. _____
2. _____
3. _____
4. _____
5. _____

today's MEALS

Meditation

What do I need to release to God today?

What am I grateful for today? Why?

What am I hearing from God today?

My successes today _____
My challenges today _____

MANIFESTATION

Did I invest in my personal growth today? ○
Did I invest in the growth of others today? ○

| AUG 14 | **MY** *Map* | ZONE ⬭ |

AGENDA | ACTIONS

6 am _____ | _____
8 am _____ | _____
9 am _____ | _____
10 am _____ | _____
11 am _____ | _____
12 pm _____ | _____
1 pm _____ | _____
2 pm _____ | _____
3 pm _____ | _____
4 pm _____ | _____
5 pm _____ | _____
6 pm _____ | _____
7 pm _____ | _____
9 pm _____ | _____

NOTES

○ AM *routine*   ○ PM *routine*

My "FAB 5" (AM)
1. _____
2. _____
3. _____
4. _____
5. _____

My "FAB 5" (PM)
1. _____
2. _____
3. _____
4. _____
5. _____

today's MEALS

Meditation

What do I need to release to God today?

What am I grateful for today? Why?

What am I hearing from God today?

My successes today _____
My challenges today _____

MANIFESTATION

Did I invest in my personal growth today? ○
Did I invest in the growth of others today? ○

| AUG 15 |

MY *Map*

ZONE

AGENDA	ACTIONS
6 am	
8 am	
9 am	
10 am	
11 am	
12 pm	
1 pm	
2 pm	
3 pm	
4 pm	
5 pm	
6 pm	
7 pm	
9 pm	

NOTES

○ AM *routine*   ○ PM *routine*

My "FAB 5" (AM)
1. _____
2. _____
3. _____
4. _____
5. _____

My "FAB 5" (PM)
1. _____
2. _____
3. _____
4. _____
5. _____

today's MEALS

Meditation

What do I need to release to God today?

What am I grateful for today? Why?

What am I hearing from God today?

My successes today _____

My challenges today _____

MANIFESTATION

Did I invest in my personal growth today? ○

Did I invest in the growth of others today? ○

| AUG 16 | MY *Map* | ZONE |

AGENDA

6 am
8 am
9 am
10 am
11 am
12 pm
1 pm
2 pm
3 pm
4 pm
5 pm
6 pm
7 pm
9 pm

ACTIONS

NOTES

○ AM *routine*   ○ PM *routine*

My "FAB 5" (AM)
1. _____
2. _____
3. _____
4. _____
5. _____

My "FAB 5" (PM)
1. _____
2. _____
3. _____
4. _____
5. _____

today's MEALS

Meditation

What do I need to release to God today?

What am I grateful for today? Why?

What am I hearing from God today?

My successes today _____
My challenges today _____

MANIFESTATION

Did I invest in my personal growth today? ○
Did I invest in the growth of others today? ○

| AUG 17 | MY *Map* | ZONE |

AGENDA

6 am
8 am
9 am
10 am
11 am
12 pm
1 pm
2 pm
3 pm
4 pm
5 pm
6 pm
7 pm
9 pm

ACTIONS

NOTES

◯ AM *routine*   ◯ PM *routine*

My "FAB 5" (AM)
1. _____
2. _____
3. _____
4. _____
5. _____

My "FAB 5" (PM)
1. _____
2. _____
3. _____
4. _____
5. _____

today's MEALS

Meditation

What do I need to release to God today?
_____

What am I grateful for today? Why?
_____

What am I hearing from God today?
_____

My successes today _____

My challenges today _____

MANIFESTATION

Did I invest in my personal growth today? ◯

Did I invest in the growth of others today? ◯

| AUG 18 | MY Map | ZONE |

AGENDA

6 am
8 am
9 am
10 am
11 am
12 pm
1 pm
2 pm
3 pm
4 pm
5 pm
6 pm
7 pm
9 pm

ACTIONS

NOTES

◯ AM *routine*   ◯ PM *routine*

My "FAB 5" (AM)
1. _____
2. _____
3. _____
4. _____
5. _____

My "FAB 5" (PM)
1. _____
2. _____
3. _____
4. _____
5. _____

today's MEALS

Meditation

What do I need to release to God today?

What am I grateful for today? Why?

What am I hearing from God today?

My successes today _____
My challenges today _____

MANIFESTATION

Did I invest in my personal growth today? ◯
Did I invest in the growth of others today? ◯

| AUG 19 | MY *Map*   ZONE

AGENDA   ACTIONS

6 am
8 am
9 am
10 am
11 am
12 pm
1 pm
2 pm
3 pm
4 pm
5 pm
6 pm
7 pm
9 pm

NOTES

◯ AM *routine*   ◯ PM *routine*

My "FAB 5" (AM)

1. _____
2. _____
3. _____
4. _____
5. _____

My "FAB 5" (PM)

1. _____
2. _____
3. _____
4. _____
5. _____

today's MEALS

Meditation

What do I need to release to God today?

What am I grateful for today? Why?

What am I hearing from God today?

My successes today _____
My challenges today _____

MANIFESTATION

Did I invest in my personal growth today? ◯
Did I invest in the growth of others today? ◯

MY Map

AUG 20 ZONE

AGENDA ACTIONS

- 6 am
- 8 am
- 9 am
- 10 am
- 11 am
- 12 pm
- 1 pm
- 2 pm
- 3 pm
- 4 pm
- 5 pm
- 6 pm
- 7 pm
- 9 pm

NOTES

◯ AM *routine*   ◯ PM *routine*

My "FAB 5" (AM)
1. _____
2. _____
3. _____
4. _____
5. _____

My "FAB 5" (PM)
1. _____
2. _____
3. _____
4. _____
5. _____

today's MEALS

Meditation

What do I need to release to God today? _____

What am I grateful for today? Why? _____

What am I hearing from God today? _____

My successes today _____
My challenges today _____

MANIFESTATION
―――――
Did I invest in my personal growth today? ◯
Did I invest in the growth of others today? ◯

| AUG 21 | MY *Map* | ZONE |

AGENDA | ACTIONS

6 am
8 am
9 am
10 am
11 am
12 pm
1 pm
2 pm
3 pm
4 pm
5 pm
6 pm
7 pm
9 pm

NOTES

○ AM *routine*   ○ PM *routine*

My "FAB 5" (AM)
1. _____
2. _____
3. _____
4. _____
5. _____

My "FAB 5" (PM)
1. _____
2. _____
3. _____
4. _____
5. _____

today's MEALS

Meditation

What do I need to release to God today?

What am I grateful for today? Why?

What am I hearing from God today?

My successes today _____
My challenges today _____

MANIFESTATION

Did I invest in my personal growth today? ○
Did I invest in the growth of others today? ○

| AUG 22 |　　　　　**MY** *Map*　　　　　| ZONE |

AGENDA　　　　　　　　ACTIONS

6 am
8 am
9 am
10 am
11 am
12 pm
1 pm
2 pm
3 pm
4 pm
5 pm
6 pm
7 pm
9 pm

NOTES

○ AM *routine*   ○ PM *routine*

My "FAB 5" (AM)
1.
2.
3.
4.
5.

My "FAB 5" (PM)
1.
2.
3.
4.
5.

today's MEALS

Meditation

What do I need to release to God today?

What am I grateful for today? Why?

What am I hearing from God today?

My successes today

My challenges today

MANIFESTATION

Did I invest in my personal growth today? ○

Did I invest in the growth of others today? ○

| AUG 23 | MY *Map* | ZONE |

AGENDA	ACTIONS
6 am	
8 am	
9 am	
10 am	
11 am	
12 pm	
1 pm	
2 pm	
3 pm	
4 pm	
5 pm	
6 pm	
7 pm	
9 pm	

NOTES

○ AM *routine*   ○ PM *routine*

My "FAB 5" (AM)
1. _____
2. _____
3. _____
4. _____
5. _____

My "FAB 5" (PM)
1. _____
2. _____
3. _____
4. _____
5. _____

today's MEALS

Meditation

What do I need to release to God today?

What am I grateful for today? Why?

What am I hearing from God today?

My successes today _____
My challenges today _____

MANIFESTATION

Did I invest in my personal growth today? ○
Did I invest in the growth of others today? ○

| AUG 24 | MY *Map* | ZONE |

AGENDA | ACTIONS

6 am

8 am

9 am

10 am

11 am

12 pm

1 pm

2 pm

3 pm

4 pm

5 pm

6 pm

7 pm

9 pm

NOTES

○ AM *routine* ○ PM *routine*

My "FAB 5" (AM)
1.
2.
3.
4.
5.

My "FAB 5" (PM)
1.
2.
3.
4.
5.

today's MEALS

Meditation

What do I need to release to God today?

What am I grateful for today? Why?

What am I hearing from God today?

My successes today
My challenges today

MANIFESTATION

Did I invest in my personal growth today? ○
Did I invest in the growth of others today? ○

| AUG 25 |

MY Map

ZONE

AGENDA

6 am
8 am
9 am
10 am
11 am
12 pm
1 pm
2 pm
3 pm
4 pm
5 pm
6 pm
7 pm
9 pm

ACTIONS

NOTES

○ AM *routine*   ○ PM *routine*

My "FAB 5" (AM)
1. _____
2. _____
3. _____
4. _____
5. _____

My "FAB 5" (PM)
1. _____
2. _____
3. _____
4. _____
5. _____

today's MEALS

Meditation

What do I need to release to God today?

What am I grateful for today? Why?

What am I hearing from God today?

My successes today _____
My challenges today _____

MANIFESTATION

Did I invest in my personal growth today? ○
Did I invest in the growth of others today? ○

AUG 26 | MY *Map* | ZONE

AGENDA

6 am
8 am
9 am
10 am
11 am
12 pm
1 pm
2 pm
3 pm
4 pm
5 pm
6 pm
7 pm
9 pm

ACTIONS

NOTES

○ AM *routine*   ○ PM *routine*

My "FAB 5" (AM)
1.
2.
3.
4.
5.

My "FAB 5" (PM)
1.
2.
3.
4.
5.

today's MEALS

Meditation

What do I need to release to God today?

What am I grateful for today? Why?

What am I hearing from God today?

My successes today

My challenges today

MANIFESTATION

Did I invest in my personal growth today? ○

Did I invest in the growth of others today? ○

MY Map

AUG 27

ZONE

AGENDA

6 am
8 am
9 am
10 am
11 am
12 pm
1 pm
2 pm
3 pm
4 pm
5 pm
6 pm
7 pm
9 pm

ACTIONS

NOTES

○ AM *routine*   ○ PM *routine*

My "FAB 5" (AM)
1. _____
2. _____
3. _____
4. _____
5. _____

My "FAB 5" (PM)
1. _____
2. _____
3. _____
4. _____
5. _____

today's MEALS

Meditation

What do I need to release to God today?

What am I grateful for today? Why?

What am I hearing from God today?

My successes today _____
My challenges today _____

MANIFESTATION

Did I invest in my personal growth today? ○
Did I invest in the growth of others today? ○

| AUG 28 |

MY Map

ZONE

AGENDA

ACTIONS

6 am
8 am
9 am
10 am
11 am
12 pm
1 pm
2 pm
3 pm
4 pm
5 pm
6 pm
7 pm
9 pm

NOTES

○ AM *routine*   ○ PM *routine*

My "FAB 5" (AM)
1. _____
2. _____
3. _____
4. _____
5. _____

My "FAB 5" (PM)
1. _____
2. _____
3. _____
4. _____
5. _____

today's MEALS

Meditation

What do I need to release to God today?
_____

What am I grateful for today? Why?
_____

What am I hearing from God today?
_____

My successes today _____
My challenges today _____

MANIFESTATION

Did I invest in my personal growth today? ○
Did I invest in the growth of others today? ○

| AUG 29 | MY Map | ZONE |

AGENDA

- 6 am
- 8 am
- 9 am
- 10 am
- 11 am
- 12 pm
- 1 pm
- 2 pm
- 3 pm
- 4 pm
- 5 pm
- 6 pm
- 7 pm
- 9 pm

ACTIONS

NOTES

○ AM *routine* ○ PM *routine*

My "FAB 5" (AM)
1. ___
2. ___
3. ___
4. ___
5. ___

My "FAB 5" (PM)
1. ___
2. ___
3. ___
4. ___
5. ___

today's MEALS

Meditation

What do I need to release to God today?

What am I grateful for today? Why?

What am I hearing from God today?

My successes today ___
My challenges today ___

MANIFESTATION

Did I invest in my personal growth today? ○
Did I invest in the growth of others today? ○

AUG 30   MY *Map*   ZONE

AGENDA	ACTIONS
6 am	
8 am	
9 am	
10 am	
11 am	
12 pm	
1 pm	
2 pm	
3 pm	
4 pm	
5 pm	
6 pm	
7 pm	
9 pm	

NOTES

○ AM *routine*   ○ PM *routine*

My "FAB 5" (AM)
1. ___
2. ___
3. ___
4. ___
5. ___

My "FAB 5" (PM)
1. ___
2. ___
3. ___
4. ___
5. ___

today's MEALS

Meditation

What do I need to release to God today?

What am I grateful for today? Why?

What am I hearing from God today?

My successes today ___
My challenges today ___

MANIFESTATION

Did I invest in my personal growth today? ○
Did I invest in the growth of others today? ○

| AUG 31 | MY *Map* | ZONE |

AGENDA

6 am
8 am
9 am
10 am
11 am
12 pm
1 pm
2 pm
3 pm
4 pm
5 pm
6 pm
7 pm
9 pm

ACTIONS

NOTES

○ AM *routine* ○ PM *routine*

My "FAB 5" (AM)
1.
2.
3.
4.
5.

My "FAB 5" (PM)
1.
2.
3.
4.
5.

today's MEALS

Meditation

What do I need to release to God today?

What am I grateful for today? Why?

What am I hearing from God today?

My successes today

My challenges today

MANIFESTATION

Did I invest in my personal growth today? ○

Did I invest in the growth of others today? ○

Attention!

Make sure you order your Q4 Master Mom Planner and schedule a personal planning session before next quarter.

Go to **www.hannahkeeley.com/planner**

| SEPT 1 | MY *Map* | ZONE |

AGENDA

6 am
8 am
9 am
10 am
11 am
12 pm
1 pm
2 pm
3 pm
4 pm
5 pm
6 pm
7 pm
9 pm

ACTIONS

NOTES

○ AM *routine*   ○ PM *routine*

My "FAB 5" (AM)
1.
2.
3.
4.
5.

My "FAB 5" (PM)
1.
2.
3.
4.
5.

today's MEALS

Meditation

What do I need to release to God today?

What am I grateful for today? Why?

What am I hearing from God today?

My successes today _____
My challenges today _____

MANIFESTATION

Did I invest in my personal growth today? ○
Did I invest in the growth of others today? ○

| SEPT 2 | MY Map | ZONE |

AGENDA

- 6 am
- 8 am
- 9 am
- 10 am
- 11 am
- 12 pm
- 1 pm
- 2 pm
- 3 pm
- 4 pm
- 5 pm
- 6 pm
- 7 pm
- 9 pm

ACTIONS

NOTES

◯ AM *routine*   ◯ PM *routine*

My "FAB 5" (AM)
1. _____
2. _____
3. _____
4. _____
5. _____

My "FAB 5" (PM)
1. _____
2. _____
3. _____
4. _____
5. _____

today's MEALS

Meditation

What do I need to release to God today?

What am I grateful for today? Why?

What am I hearing from God today?

My successes today _____
My challenges today _____

MANIFESTATION

Did I invest in my personal growth today? ◯
Did I invest in the growth of others today? ◯

SEPT 3

MY Map

ZONE

AGENDA

6 am

8 am

9 am

10 am

11 am

12 pm

1 pm

2 pm

3 pm

4 pm

5 pm

6 pm

7 pm

9 pm

ACTIONS

NOTES

○ AM *routine*   ○ PM *routine*

My "FAB 5" (AM)
1. _____
2. _____
3. _____
4. _____
5. _____

My "FAB 5" (PM)
1. _____
2. _____
3. _____
4. _____
5. _____

today's MEALS

Meditation

What do I need to release to God today?

What am I grateful for today? Why?

What am I hearing from God today?

My successes today _____
My challenges today _____

MANIFESTATION

Did I invest in my personal growth today? ○
Did I invest in the growth of others today? ○

SEPT 4   MY *Map*   ZONE

AGENDA

6 am
8 am
9 am
10 am
11 am
12 pm
1 pm
2 pm
3 pm
4 pm
5 pm
6 pm
7 pm
9 pm

ACTIONS

NOTES

○ AM *routine*   ○ PM *routine*

My "FAB 5" (AM)
1. _____
2. _____
3. _____
4. _____
5. _____

My "FAB 5" (PM)
1. _____
2. _____
3. _____
4. _____
5. _____

today's MEALS

Meditation

What do I need to release to God today?

What am I grateful for today? Why?

What am I hearing from God today?

My successes today _____
My challenges today _____

MANIFESTATION

Did I invest in my personal growth today? ○
Did I invest in the growth of others today? ○

SEPT 5

MY Map

ZONE

AGENDA

6 am
8 am
9 am
10 am
11 am
12 pm
1 pm
2 pm
3 pm
4 pm
5 pm
6 pm
7 pm
9 pm

ACTIONS

NOTES

○ AM *routine*   ○ PM *routine*

My "FAB 5" (AM)
1. ___
2. ___
3. ___
4. ___
5. ___

My "FAB 5" (PM)
1. ___
2. ___
3. ___
4. ___
5. ___

today's MEALS

Meditation

What do I need to release to God today?

What am I grateful for today? Why?

What am I hearing from God today?

My successes today ___
My challenges today ___

MANIFESTATION

Did I invest in my personal growth today? ○
Did I invest in the growth of others today? ○

SEPT 6 — MY *Map* — ZONE

AGENDA

- 6 am
- 8 am
- 9 am
- 10 am
- 11 am
- 12 pm
- 1 pm
- 2 pm
- 3 pm
- 4 pm
- 5 pm
- 6 pm
- 7 pm
- 9 pm

ACTIONS

NOTES

○ AM *routine*   ○ PM *routine*

My "FAB 5" (AM)
1. _____
2. _____
3. _____
4. _____
5. _____

My "FAB 5" (PM)
1. _____
2. _____
3. _____
4. _____
5. _____

today's MEALS

Meditation

What do I need to release to God today?

What am I grateful for today? Why?

What am I hearing from God today?

My successes today _____
My challenges today _____

MANIFESTATION

Did I invest in my personal growth today?   ○
Did I invest in the growth of others today? ○

SEPT 7   MY *Map*   ZONE

AGENDA	ACTIONS
6 am	
8 am	
9 am	
10 am	
11 am	
12 pm	
1 pm	
2 pm	
3 pm	
4 pm	
5 pm	
6 pm	
7 pm	
9 pm	

NOTES

○ AM *routine*   ○ PM *routine*

My "FAB 5" (AM)
1. _____
2. _____
3. _____
4. _____
5. _____

My "FAB 5" (PM)
1. _____
2. _____
3. _____
4. _____
5. _____

today's MEALS

Meditation

What do I need to release to God today?

What am I grateful for today? Why?

What am I hearing from God today?

My successes today _____
My challenges today _____

MANIFESTATION

Did I invest in my personal growth today? ○
Did I invest in the growth of others today? ○

(SEPT 8)

MY *Map*

ZONE (   )

AGENDA

6 am
8 am
9 am
10 am
11 am
12 pm
1 pm
2 pm
3 pm
4 pm
5 pm
6 pm
7 pm
9 pm

ACTIONS

NOTES

○ AM *routine* ○ PM *routine*

My "FAB 5" (AM)
1.
2.
3.
4.
5.

My "FAB 5" (PM)
1.
2.
3.
4.
5.

today's MEALS

Meditation

What do I need to release to God today?

What am I grateful for today? Why?

What am I hearing from God today?

My successes today

My challenges today

MANIFESTATION

Did I invest in my personal growth today? ○

Did I invest in the growth of others today? ○

SEPT 9 | MY *Map* | ZONE

AGENDA

- 6 am
- 8 am
- 9 am
- 10 am
- 11 am
- 12 pm
- 1 pm
- 2 pm
- 3 pm
- 4 pm
- 5 pm
- 6 pm
- 7 pm
- 9 pm

ACTIONS

NOTES

○ AM *routine*   ○ PM *routine*

My "FAB 5" (AM)
1. ___
2. ___
3. ___
4. ___
5. ___

My "FAB 5" (PM)
1. ___
2. ___
3. ___
4. ___
5. ___

today's MEALS

Meditation

What do I need to release to God today?

What am I grateful for today? Why?

What am I hearing from God today?

My successes today ___
My challenges today ___

MANIFESTATION

Did I invest in my personal growth today? ○
Did I invest in the growth of others today? ○

| SEPT 10 | MY *Map* | ZONE |

AGENDA

6 am
8 am
9 am
10 am
11 am
12 pm
1 pm
2 pm
3 pm
4 pm
5 pm
6 pm
7 pm
9 pm

ACTIONS

NOTES

○ AM *routine*   ○ PM *routine*

My "FAB 5" (AM)
1. _____
2. _____
3. _____
4. _____
5. _____

My "FAB 5" (PM)
1. _____
2. _____
3. _____
4. _____
5. _____

today's MEALS

Meditation

What do I need to release to God today?

What am I grateful for today? Why?

What am I hearing from God today?

My successes today _____
My challenges today _____

MANIFESTATION

Did I invest in my personal growth today? ○
Did I invest in the growth of others today? ○

SEPT 11 — MY *Map* — ZONE

AGENDA

- 6 am
- 8 am
- 9 am
- 10 am
- 11 am
- 12 pm
- 1 pm
- 2 pm
- 3 pm
- 4 pm
- 5 pm
- 6 pm
- 7 pm
- 9 pm

ACTIONS

NOTES

○ AM *routine*   ○ PM *routine*

My "FAB 5" (AM)
1. _____
2. _____
3. _____
4. _____
5. _____

My "FAB 5" (PM)
1. _____
2. _____
3. _____
4. _____
5. _____

today's MEALS

Meditation

What do I need to release to God today?

What am I grateful for today? Why?

What am I hearing from God today?

My successes today _____
My challenges today _____

MANIFESTATION

Did I invest in my personal growth today? ○
Did I invest in the growth of others today? ○

SEPT 12 MY *Map* ZONE

AGENDA

6 am
8 am
9 am
10 am
11 am
12 pm
1 pm
2 pm
3 pm
4 pm
5 pm
6 pm
7 pm
9 pm

ACTIONS

NOTES

○ AM *routine*   ○ PM *routine*

My "FAB 5" (AM)
1. _____
2. _____
3. _____
4. _____
5. _____

My "FAB 5" (PM)
1. _____
2. _____
3. _____
4. _____
5. _____

today's MEALS

Meditation

What do I need to release to God today?

What am I grateful for today? Why?

What am I hearing from God today?

My successes today _____
My challenges today _____

MANIFESTATION

Did I invest in my personal growth today? ○
Did I invest in the growth of others today? ○

| SEPT 13 | MY *Map* | ZONE |

AGENDA

- 6 am
- 8 am
- 9 am
- 10 am
- 11 am
- 12 pm
- 1 pm
- 2 pm
- 3 pm
- 4 pm
- 5 pm
- 6 pm
- 7 pm
- 9 pm

ACTIONS

NOTES

○ AM *routine*   ○ PM *routine*

My "FAB 5" (AM)
1.
2.
3.
4.
5.

My "FAB 5" (PM)
1.
2.
3.
4.
5.

today's MEALS

Meditation

What do I need to release to God today?

What am I grateful for today? Why?

What am I hearing from God today?

My successes today
My challenges today

MANIFESTATION

Did I invest in my personal growth today? ○
Did I invest in the growth of others today? ○

SEPT 14   MY *Map*   ZONE

AGENDA

6 am
8 am
9 am
10 am
11 am
12 pm
1 pm
2 pm
3 pm
4 pm
5 pm
6 pm
7 pm
9 pm

ACTIONS

NOTES

○ AM *routine*   ○ PM *routine*

My "FAB 5" (AM)
1. _____
2. _____
3. _____
4. _____
5. _____

My "FAB 5" (PM)
1. _____
2. _____
3. _____
4. _____
5. _____

today's MEALS

Meditation

What do I need to release to God today?

What am I grateful for today? Why?

What am I hearing from God today?

My successes today _____
My challenges today _____

MANIFESTATION

Did I invest in my personal growth today? ○
Did I invest in the growth of others today? ○

| SEPT 15 | MY *Map* | ZONE |

AGENDA | ACTIONS

6 am
8 am
9 am
10 am
11 am
12 pm
1 pm
2 pm
3 pm
4 pm
5 pm
6 pm
7 pm
9 pm

NOTES

○ AM *routine*   ○ PM *routine*

My "FAB 5" (AM)
1.
2.
3.
4.
5.

My "FAB 5" (PM)
1.
2.
3.
4.
5.

today's MEALS

Meditation

What do I need to release to God today?

What am I grateful for today? Why?

What am I hearing from God today?

My successes today

My challenges today

MANIFESTATION

Did I invest in my personal growth today? ○

Did I invest in the growth of others today? ○

SEPT 16 MY *Map* ZONE

AGENDA

- 6 am
- 8 am
- 9 am
- 10 am
- 11 am
- 12 pm
- 1 pm
- 2 pm
- 3 pm
- 4 pm
- 5 pm
- 6 pm
- 7 pm
- 9 pm

ACTIONS

NOTES

○ AM *routine*   ○ PM *routine*

My "FAB 5" (AM)
1. _____
2. _____
3. _____
4. _____
5. _____

My "FAB 5" (PM)
1. _____
2. _____
3. _____
4. _____
5. _____

today's MEALS

Meditation

What do I need to release to God today?

What am I grateful for today? Why?

What am I hearing from God today?

My successes today _____

My challenges today _____

MANIFESTATION

Did I invest in my personal growth today? ○

Did I invest in the growth of others today? ○

SEPT 17 MY *Map* ZONE

AGENDA

6 am
8 am
9 am
10 am
11 am
12 pm
1 pm
2 pm
3 pm
4 pm
5 pm
6 pm
7 pm
9 pm

ACTIONS

NOTES

○ AM *routine*   ○ PM *routine*

My "FAB 5" (AM)
1. _____
2. _____
3. _____
4. _____
5. _____

My "FAB 5" (PM)
1. _____
2. _____
3. _____
4. _____
5. _____

today's MEALS

Meditation

What do I need to release to God today?

What am I grateful for today? Why?

What am I hearing from God today?

My successes today _____

My challenges today _____

MANIFESTATION

Did I invest in my personal growth today? ○

Did I invest in the growth of others today? ○

SEPT 18		MY *Map*		ZONE

AGENDA

- 6 am
- 8 am
- 9 am
- 10 am
- 11 am
- 12 pm
- 1 pm
- 2 pm
- 3 pm
- 4 pm
- 5 pm
- 6 pm
- 7 pm
- 9 pm

ACTIONS

NOTES

◯ AM *routine*　　◯ PM *routine*

My "FAB 5" (AM)
1. _____
2. _____
3. _____
4. _____
5. _____

My "FAB 5" (PM)
1. _____
2. _____
3. _____
4. _____
5. _____

today's MEALS

Meditation

What do I need to release to God today?

What am I grateful for today? Why?

What am I hearing from God today?

My successes today _____
My challenges today _____

MANIFESTATION

Did I invest in my personal growth today?　◯
Did I invest in the growth of others today?　◯

| SEPT 19 | MY *Map* | ZONE |

AGENDA

ACTIONS

6 am

8 am

9 am

10 am

11 am

12 pm

1 pm

2 pm

3 pm

4 pm

5 pm

6 pm

7 pm

9 pm

NOTES

◯ AM *routine*   ◯ PM *routine*

My "FAB 5" (AM)
1. _____
2. _____
3. _____
4. _____
5. _____

My "FAB 5" (PM)
1. _____
2. _____
3. _____
4. _____
5. _____

today's MEALS

Meditation

What do I need to release to God today?

What am I grateful for today? Why?

What am I hearing from God today?

My successes today _____
My challenges today _____

MANIFESTATION

Did I invest in my personal growth today? ◯
Did I invest in the growth of others today? ◯

MY Map

SEPT 20 ZONE

AGENDA

6 am
8 am
9 am
10 am
11 am
12 pm
1 pm
2 pm
3 pm
4 pm
5 pm
6 pm
7 pm
9 pm

ACTIONS

NOTES

◯ AM *routine*   ◯ PM *routine*

My "FAB 5" (AM)
1. _____
2. _____
3. _____
4. _____
5. _____

My "FAB 5" (PM)
1. _____
2. _____
3. _____
4. _____
5. _____

today's MEALS

Meditation

What do I need to release to God today?

What am I grateful for today? Why?

What am I hearing from God today?

My successes today _____
My challenges today _____

MANIFESTATION

Did I invest in my personal growth today? ◯
Did I invest in the growth of others today? ◯

| SEPT 21 | MY *Map* | ZONE |

AGENDA

6 am
8 am
9 am
10 am
11 am
12 pm
1 pm
2 pm
3 pm
4 pm
5 pm
6 pm
7 pm
9 pm

ACTIONS

NOTES

○ AM *routine*   ○ PM *routine*

My "FAB 5" (AM)
1. ___
2. ___
3. ___
4. ___
5. ___

My "FAB 5" (PM)
1. ___
2. ___
3. ___
4. ___
5. ___

today's MEALS

Meditation

What do I need to release to God today?

What am I grateful for today? Why?

What am I hearing from God today?

My successes today ___
My challenges today ___

MANIFESTATION

Did I invest in my personal growth today? ○
Did I invest in the growth of others today? ○

SEPT 22 — MY Map — ZONE

AGENDA

6 am
8 am
9 am
10 am
11 am
12 pm
1 pm
2 pm
3 pm
4 pm
5 pm
6 pm
7 pm
9 pm

ACTIONS

NOTES

◯ AM *routine*   ◯ PM *routine*

My "FAB 5" (AM)
1.
2.
3.
4.
5.

My "FAB 5" (PM)
1.
2.
3.
4.
5.

today's MEALS

Meditation

What do I need to release to God today?

What am I grateful for today? Why?

What am I hearing from God today?

My successes today

My challenges today

MANIFESTATION

Did I invest in my personal growth today?   ◯
Did I invest in the growth of others today?   ◯

SEPT 23 — MY *Map* — ZONE

AGENDA

6 am
8 am
9 am
10 am
11 am
12 pm
1 pm
2 pm
3 pm
4 pm
5 pm
6 pm
7 pm
9 pm

ACTIONS

NOTES

○ AM *routine*   ○ PM *routine*

My "FAB 5" (AM)
1. _____
2. _____
3. _____
4. _____
5. _____

My "FAB 5" (PM)
1. _____
2. _____
3. _____
4. _____
5. _____

today's MEALS

Meditation

What do I need to release to God today?

What am I grateful for today? Why?

What am I hearing from God today?

My successes today _____
My challenges today _____

MANIFESTATION

Did I invest in my personal growth today? ○
Did I invest in the growth of others today? ○

| SEPT 24 |

MY Map

ZONE

AGENDA

6 am
8 am
9 am
10 am
11 am
12 pm
1 pm
2 pm
3 pm
4 pm
5 pm
6 pm
7 pm
9 pm

ACTIONS

NOTES

200

○ AM *routine*   ○ PM *routine*

My "FAB 5" (AM)
1. _____
2. _____
3. _____
4. _____
5. _____

My "FAB 5" (PM)
1. _____
2. _____
3. _____
4. _____
5. _____

today's MEALS

Meditation

What do I need to release to God today?

What am I grateful for today? Why?

What am I hearing from God today?

My successes today _____
My challenges today _____

MANIFESTATION

Did I invest in my personal growth today? ○
Did I invest in the growth of others today? ○

MY *Map*

SEPT 25 ZONE

AGENDA

- 6 am
- 8 am
- 9 am
- 10 am
- 11 am
- 12 pm
- 1 pm
- 2 pm
- 3 pm
- 4 pm
- 5 pm
- 6 pm
- 7 pm
- 9 pm

ACTIONS

NOTES

◯ AM *routine*   ◯ PM *routine*

My "FAB 5" (AM)
1.
2.
3.
4.
5.

My "FAB 5" (PM)
1.
2.
3.
4.
5.

today's MEALS

Meditation

What do I need to release to God today?

What am I grateful for today? Why?

What am I hearing from God today?

My successes today
My challenges today

MANIFESTATION

Did I invest in my personal growth today? ◯
Did I invest in the growth of others today? ◯

SEPT 26 MY *Map* ZONE

AGENDA | ACTIONS

6 am
8 am
9 am
10 am
11 am
12 pm
1 pm
2 pm
3 pm
4 pm
5 pm
6 pm
7 pm
9 pm

NOTES

○ AM *routine*   ○ PM *routine*

My "FAB 5" (AM)
1. _____
2. _____
3. _____
4. _____
5. _____

My "FAB 5" (PM)
1. _____
2. _____
3. _____
4. _____
5. _____

today's MEALS

Meditation

What do I need to release to God today?

What am I grateful for today? Why?

What am I hearing from God today?

My successes today _____
My challenges today _____

MANIFESTATION

Did I invest in my personal growth today? ○
Did I invest in the growth of others today? ○

SEPT 27

MY Map

ZONE

AGENDA

6 am
8 am
9 am
10 am
11 am
12 pm
1 pm
2 pm
3 pm
4 pm
5 pm
6 pm
7 pm
9 pm

ACTIONS

NOTES

○ AM *routine* ○ PM *routine*

My "FAB 5" (AM)
1. _____
2. _____
3. _____
4. _____
5. _____

My "FAB 5" (PM)
1. _____
2. _____
3. _____
4. _____
5. _____

today's MEALS

Meditation

What do I need to release to God today?

What am I grateful for today? Why?

What am I hearing from God today?

My successes today _____
My challenges today _____

MANIFESTATION

Did I invest in my personal growth today? ○
Did I invest in the growth of others today? ○

| SEPT 28 | MY Map | ZONE |

AGENDA | ACTIONS

- 6 am
- 8 am
- 9 am
- 10 am
- 11 am
- 12 pm
- 1 pm
- 2 pm
- 3 pm
- 4 pm
- 5 pm
- 6 pm
- 7 pm
- 9 pm

NOTES

○ AM *routine* ○ PM *routine*

My "FAB 5" (AM)
1. _____
2. _____
3. _____
4. _____
5. _____

My "FAB 5" (PM)
1. _____
2. _____
3. _____
4. _____
5. _____

today's MEALS

Meditation

What do I need to release to God today?

What am I grateful for today? Why?

What am I hearing from God today?

My successes today _____
My challenges today _____

MANIFESTATION

Did I invest in my personal growth today? ○
Did I invest in the growth of others today? ○

SEPT 29 — MY *Map* — ZONE

AGENDA

- 6 am
- 8 am
- 9 am
- 10 am
- 11 am
- 12 pm
- 1 pm
- 2 pm
- 3 pm
- 4 pm
- 5 pm
- 6 pm
- 7 pm
- 9 pm

ACTIONS

NOTES

○ AM *routine*   ○ PM *routine*

My "FAB 5" (AM)
1. _____
2. _____
3. _____
4. _____
5. _____

My "FAB 5" (PM)
1. _____
2. _____
3. _____
4. _____
5. _____

today's MEALS

Meditation

What do I need to release to God today?

What am I grateful for today? Why?

What am I hearing from God today?

My successes today _____
My challenges today _____

MANIFESTATION

Did I invest in my personal growth today? ○
Did I invest in the growth of others today? ○

SEPT 30 | MY Map | ZONE

AGENDA

6 am
8 am
9 am
10 am
11 am
12 pm
1 pm
2 pm
3 pm
4 pm
5 pm
6 pm
7 pm
9 pm

ACTIONS

NOTES

○ AM *routine* ○ PM *routine*

My "FAB 5" (AM)
1. _____
2. _____
3. _____
4. _____
5. _____

My "FAB 5" (PM)
1. _____
2. _____
3. _____
4. _____
5. _____

today's MEALS

Meditation

What do I need to release to God today?

What am I grateful for today? Why?

What am I hearing from God today?

My successes today _____
My challenges today _____

MANIFESTATION

Did I invest in my personal growth today? ○
Did I invest in the growth of others today? ○

Made in the USA
Columbia, SC
02 September 2024